All for Love

All for Love

A ROMANTIC ANTHOLOGY

LAURA STODDART

CHRONICLE BOOKS
SAN FRANCISCO

For Camilla

First published in the United States of America in 2008 by Chronicle Books LLC.
First published in Great Britain in 2007 by Orion Publishing Group Ltd.

Illustrations and text selection copyright © 2007 by Laura Stoddart.

Library of Congress Cataloging-in-Publication Data available.

ISBN-10: 0-8118-6100-7
ISBN-13: 978-0-8118-6100-7

Manufactured in Italy
Researched by Jane Fior and Camilla Stoddart

10 9 8 7 6 5 4 3 2 1

Chronicle Books LLC
680 Second Street
San Francisco, California 94107

www.chroniclebooks.com

CONTENTS

What thing is love? for well I wot, love is a thing,
It is a prick, it is a sting,
It is a pretty pretty thing;
It is a fire, it is a coal,
Whose flame creeps in at every hole;
And as my wit doth best devise,
Love's dwelling is in ladies' eyes:
From whence do glance love's piercing darts
That make such holes into our hearts;
And all the world herein accord
Love is a great and mighty lord,
And when he list to mount so high,
With Venus he in heaven doth lie,
Since Mars and she played even and odd.

George Peele (1588–1596)

PART I
The Nature of Love

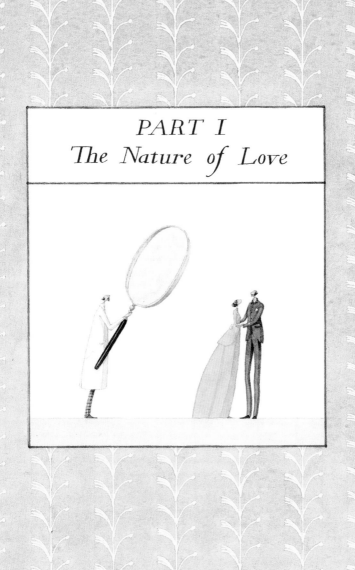

And even so, what happiness to be loved! And, oh you gods, what happiness it is to love!

Johann Wolfgang von Goethe (1749–1832) *Wilkommen und Abschied*

He that hath love in his breast hath spurs in his sides.

Anonymous

'Love,' she said, 'seems to pump me full of vitamins. It makes me feel as if the sun were shining and my hat was right and my shoes were right and my frock was right and my stockings were right, and somebody had just left me ten thousand a year.'

P G Wodehouse (1881–1975) *Spring Fever*

I shall be great and you rich, because we love each other.

Victor Hugo (1802–1885) *Un Peu de Musique*

Shall I compare thee to a summer's day?
Thou are more lovely and more temperate.
Rough winds do shake the darling buds of May,
And summer's lease hath all too short a date.

William Shakespeare (1564–1616) Sonnet 18

You!

Gavin Ewart (1916–1955) 'The Lover Writes a One-Word Poem'

Love; that self-love *a deux*.

Madame de Stael (1766–1817)

How do I love thee? Let me count the ways.
I love thee to the depth and breadth and height
My soul can reach.

Elizabeth Barrett Browning (1806–1861) Sonnets from the Portuguese

Oh, my Luve's like a red red rose
That's newly sprung in June:
O, my Luve's like the melodie
That's sweetly play'd in tune.

Robert Burns (1759–1796)

Let us live, my Lesbia, and let us love, and let us value all the
mutterings of grumpy old men at just a farthing.

Catullus (c87–c54 BC)

O Love, how thou are tired out with rhyme!
Thou art a tree whereon all poets clime.

Margaret Cavendish, Duchess of Newcastle (1624–1674) 'Love and Poetry'

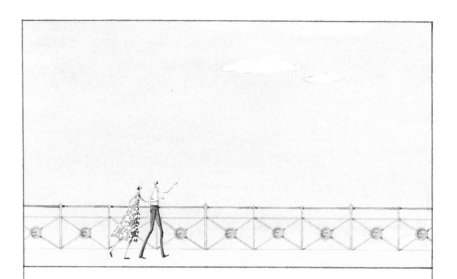

When love comes it comes without effort, like perfect weather.

Helen Yglesias *Family Feeling*

Faith is like love: neither can be forced.

Johann Wolfgang von Goethe (1749–1832)

Love gives naught but itself and takes naught but from itself.
Love possesses not nor would it be possessed;
For love is sufficient unto love.

Kahlil Gibran (1883–1931) *The Prophet*

Let me not to the marriage of true minds
Admit impediments. Love is not love
Which alters when it alteration finds,
Or bends with the remover to remove:
O, no! it is an ever-fixed mark.

William Shakespeare (1564–1616) *Sonnet 116*

Love keeps out the cold better than a cloak.

Anonymous

Love looks not with the eyes, but with the mind,
And therefore is winged Cupid painted blind.

William Shakespeare (1564–1616) *A Midsummer Night's Dream*

Love can beauties spy
In what seem faults to every common eye.

John Gay (1685–1732)

Credula res amor est (in love you'll believe anything).

Anonymous

Thou hast no faults
Or none that I can spy.
Thou art all sweetness,
Or, all blindness I.

Anonymous

To be together is for us at once to be as free as in solitude, as gay as in company. We talk, I believe, all day long: to talk to each other is but a more animated and an audible thinking.

Charlotte Bronte (1816–1855) *Jane Eyre*

To love deeply in one direction makes us more loving in all others.

Anne-Sophie Swetchine (1788–1857)

Whatever our souls are made of, his and mine are the same.

Emily Bronte (1818–1848) *Wuthering Heights*

If I were pressed to say why I loved him, I feel that my only reply could be: 'Because it was he, because it was I'.

Michel de Montaigne (1533–1592) *Essays*

I love you more than yesterday, less than tomorrow.

Edmond Rostand (1868–1918) *Les Musardise*

Love – bittersweet, irrepressible –
Loosens my limbs and I tremble.

Sappho (650–590 BC) 'To Athis'

Love, when we are in your grip, we may well say, Farewell,
caution.

Jean de la Fontaine (1621–1695) 'Le Lion Amoureux'

L'amour est un oiseau rebelle.

Prosper Merimée (1803–1870) *Carmen*

We don't believe in rheumatism or true love until we have been
attacked by them.

Marie von Ebner-Eschenbach (1830–1916) *Aphorisms*

Militiae species amoris
Love is a kind of warfare.

Ovid (43BC–AD17)

For aught that I could read
Could ever hear by tale or history,
The course of true love never did run smooth.

William Shakespeare (1564–1616) *A Midsummer Night's Dream*

That arch-disturber of tranquillity . . . Love, waylayer of all hearts.

Gottfried von Strassburg (13th century)

Pains of love be sweeter far
Than all other pleasures are.

John Dryden (1631–1700)

The absolute yearning of one human body for another particular one and its indifference to substitutes is one of life's major mysteries.

Iris Murdoch (1918–1999) *The Black Prince*

Shall I, wasting in despair,
Die because a woman's fair?

George Wither (1588–1667)

I'm glad it cannot happen twice, the fever of first love.

Daphne du Maurier (1907–1989) *Rebecca*

Love is like the measles; we all have to go through it.

Jerome K Jerome (1859–1927) *Idle Thoughts of an Idle Fellow*

The magic of first love is our ignorance that it can ever end.

Benjamin Disraeli (1804–1881)

Birds do it, bees do it,
Even educated fleas do it,
Let's do it, let's fall in love.

The ancient Romans and the Greeks did it,
Even nice young men who sell antiques do it,
Let's do it, let's fall in love . . .

Cole Porter (1891–1964) 'Let's Do It'

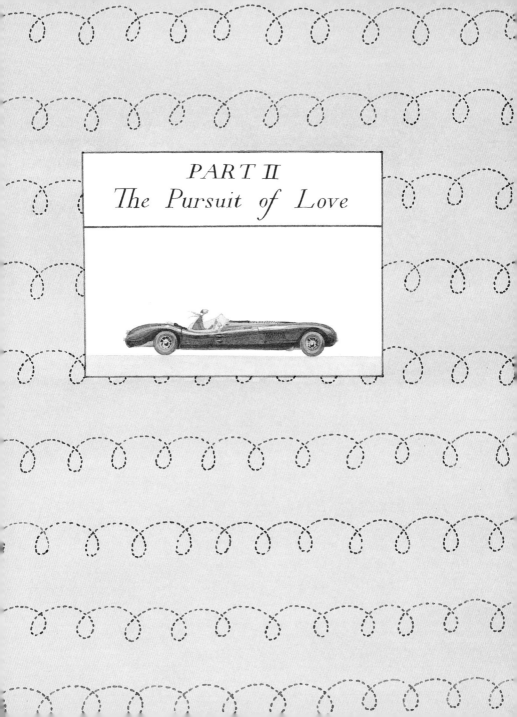

PART II
The Pursuit of Love

A young man and a young woman in a green arbour on a May morning – if God would not forgive it, I would.

Sir John Harington (1561–1612)

It was a lover and his lass
With a hey, and a ho, and a hey nonino,
That o'er the green cornfield did pass,
In the spring time, the only pretty ring time,
When birds do sing, hey ding a ding, ding;
Sweet lovers love the spring.

William Shakespeare (1564–1616) *As You Like It*

In the spring a young man's fancy
Lightly turns to thoughts of love.

Alfred, Lord Tennyson (1809–1892) *Locksley Hall*

Let us now bask under the spreading trees said Bernard in a passionate tone. Oh yes lets said Ethel and she opened her dainty parasole and sank down upon the long grass. She closed her eyes but she was far from asleep.

Daisy Ashford (aged 9) (1881–1972) *The Young Visiters*

Because women can do nothing except love, they've given it
a ridiculous importance.

Somerset Maugham (1874–1965) *The Moon and Sixpence*

Lively, ingenuous, conversable and charming little girls often spoil
into dull, bashful, silent young ladies, and all because their heads
are full of nonsense about beaux and lovers.

Anonymous *How to Woo, or The Etiquette of Courtship* (1879)

Next to being married, a girl likes to be crossed a little now
and then.

Jane Austen (1775–1817) *Pride and Prejudice*

She's got most of the symptoms – is twittery and cross, doesn't
eat, lies awake, and mopes in corners.

Louisa May Alcott (1832–1888) *Little Women*

In all the woes that curse our race
There is a lady in the case.

W S Gilbert (1836–1911) 'Fallen Fairies'

When a man is really in love he can't help looking like a sheep.

Agatha Christie (1890–1976) *The Mystery of the Blue Train*

His eyes were rolling in their sockets, and his face had taken on
the colour and expression of a devout tomato. I could see that he
loved her like a thousand bricks.

P G Wodehouse (1881–1975) *Joy in the Morning*

I am in love and I want to grow pale; I am in love and
I want to suffer; I am in love, and I give away my genius
in exchange for a kiss.

Alfred de Musset (1810–1857) *La Nuit d'Aout*

What kind of business is this? The bed is hard and the covers
Will not stay in their place; I thrash and I toss, and I turn
All the long night through, till my bones are utterly weary.
What's the matter with me? Am I a victim of love?

Ovid (43BC–AD17)

Love has unbound my limbs and set me shaking,
A monster bitter sweet and my unmaking.

Sappho (650–590BC)

You know how you ought to be with men? You should always be aloof, you should never let them know you like them, you must on no account let them feel that they are of any importance to you, you must be wrapped up in your own concerns, you may never let them lose sight of the fact that you are superior, you must be, in short, a regular stuffed chemise.

Dorothy Parker (1893–1967) *Wallflower's Lament*

One has no sooner left off one's bib and apron, than people cry – 'Miss will soon be married!' – and this man, and that man, is presently picked out for a husband. Mighty ridiculous! They want to deprive us of all the pleasures of life, just when one begins to have a relish for them.

Eliza Haywood (1693–1756) *The History of Miss Betty Thoughtless*

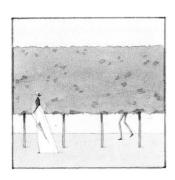

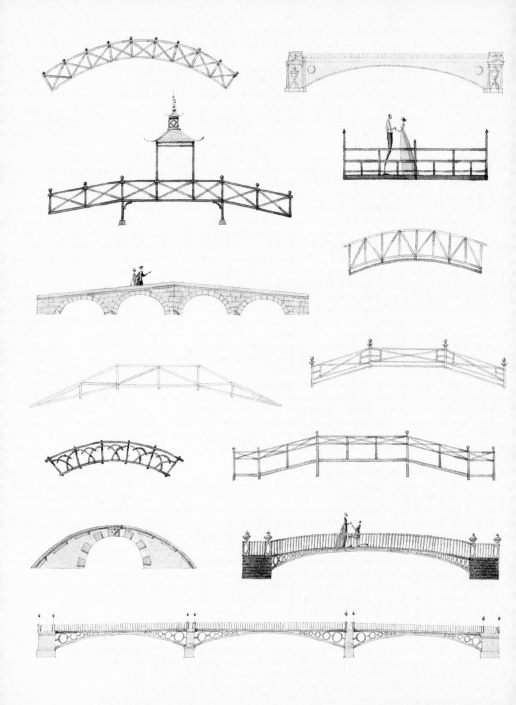

Many a man has fallen in love with a girl in a light so dim he would not have chosen a suit by it.

Maurice Chevalier (1888–1972) *News Summaries*

'I'd be crazy to propose to her, but when I see that profile of hers I feel that the only thing worth doing in the world is to grab her and start shouting for clergymen and bridesmaids to come running.'

P G Wodehouse (1881–1975) *Plum Pie*

'Mr Collins, you must marry. – Chuse properly, chuse a gentlewoman for my sake; and for your *own*, let her be an active, useful sort of person . . . able to make a small income go a good way.'

Jane Austen (1775–1817) *Pride and Prejudice*

I . . . chose my wife, as she did her wedding gown, not for a fine glossy surface, but for such qualities as would wear well.

Oliver Goldsmith (1728–1774) *The Vicar of Wakefield*

29

I really don't see anything romantic in proposing. It is very romantic to be in love. But there is nothing romantic about a definite proposal. Why, one may be accepted. One usually is, I believe. Then the excitement is all over. The very essence is uncertainty.

Oscar Wilde (1854–1900) *The Importance of Being Earnest*

Courtship to marriage, as a very witty prologue to a very dull play.

William Congreve (1670–1729) *The Old Bachelor*

A lady's imagination is very rapid; it jumps from admiration to love, from love to matrimony in a moment.

Jane Austen (1775–1817) *Pride and Prejudice*

'It's got so nowadays,' said Ukridge, with a strong sense of injury, 'that you've only got to throw a girl a kindly word, and the next thing you know you're in the Lord Warden at Dover, picking the rice out of your hair.'

P G Wodehouse (1881–1975) *Ukridge*

For talk six times with the same single lady,
And you may get the wedding dresses ready.

George Gordon, Lord Byron (1788–1824) *Don Juan*

Romances paint a full length people's wooings,
    But only give a bust for marriages:
For no one cares for matrimonial cooings,
    There's nothing wrong in a connubial kiss.
Think you, if Laura had been Petrarch's wife,
He would have written sonnets all his life?

George Gordon, Lord Byron (1788–1824) *Don Juan*

PART III
Love and Marriage

Hogamus, higamus,
Man is polygamous;
Higamus, hogamus,
Woman's monogamous.

Anonymous

Warm though the morning was, he shivered, as only a confirmed bachelor gazing into the naked face of matrimony can shiver.

P G Wodehouse (1881–1975) *The Old Reliable*

Marriage is an attempt to turn a night owl into a homing pigeon.

Anonymous

You may carve it on his tombstone, you may cut it on his card,
That a young man married is a young man marred.

Rudyard Kipling (1865–1936) 'The Story of the Gadsbys'

I should like to know what is the proper function of women, if it is not to make reasons for husbands to stay at home, and still stronger reasons for bachelors to go out.

George Eliot (1819–1880) *The Mill on the Floss*

Is not marriage an open question, when it is alleged, from the beginning of the world, that such as are in the institution wish to get out; and such as are out wish to get in?

Ralph Waldo Emerson (1803–1882) *Representative Men*

It is a woman's business to get married as soon as possible, and a man's to keep unmarried as long as he can.

George Bernard Shaw (1856–1950) *Major Barbara*

Because what if I'm 60 years old and not married.
All alone in a furnished room with pee stains on my underwear and everyone else is married! All the universe married but me!

Gregory Corso (1930–2001) 'Marriage'

One [woman] is pretty nearly as good as another, as far as any judgement can be formed of them before marriage. It is only after marriage that they show their true qualities, as I know from bitter experience. Marriage is, therefore, a lottery and the less choice and selection a man bestows on his ticket the better.

Thomas Love Peacock (1785–1866) *Nightmare Abbey*

It doesn't much signify whom one marries, for one is sure to find out next morning that it was someone else.

Samuel Rogers (1763–1855) *Table Talk*

Remember, it is as easy to marry a rich woman as a poor woman.

William Makepeace Thackeray (1811–1863) *Pendennis*

'Chumps always make the best husbands. When you marry, Sally, grab a chump. Tap his forehead first, and if it rings solid, don't hesitate.'

P G Wodehouse (1881–1975) *The Adventures of Sally*

Why have such scores of lovely, gifted girls
Married impossible men?

Robert Graves (1895–1985) 'A Slice of Wedding-Cake'

An archaeologist is the best husband any woman can have: the older she gets, the more interested he is in her.

Dame Agatha Christie (1890–1976)

Reader, I married him.

Charlotte Bronte (1816–1855) *Jane Eyre*

Meek wifehood is no part of my profession:
I am your friend, but never your possession.

Vera Brittain (1893–1970) 'Married Love'

Strange to say what delight we married people have
to see these poor fools decoyed into our condition.

Samuel Pepys (1633–1703) *Diary*

Nothing is to me more distasteful than that entire
complacency and satisfaction which beam in the
countenance of a new-married couple.

Charles Lamb (1775–1834)
'A Bachelor's Complaint of Married People'

Marriage may often be a stormy lake, but celibacy is almost always a muddy horsepond.

Thomas Love Peacock (1785–1866) *Melincourt*

The best part of married life is the fights. The rest is merely so-so.

Thornton Wilder (1897–1975) *The Matchmaker*

When you're away, I'm restless, lonely,
Wretched, bored, dejected; only
Here's the rub, my darling dear,
I feel the same when you are near.

Samuel Hoffenstein (1890–1947)

Even quarrels with one's husband are preferable to the ennui of a solitary existence.

Elizabeth Patterson Bonaparte (1785–1879)

The comfortable estate of widowhood is the only hope that keeps up a wife's spirits.

John Gay (1685–1732) *The Beggar's Opera*

If you cannot have your dear husband for a comfort and a delight, for a breadwinner and a crosspatch, for a sofa, chair or hot-water bottle, one can use him as a Cross to be borne.

Stevie Smith (1902–1971) *Novel on Yellow Paper*

How to be Happy Though Married

Title of book by the Rev E J Hardy (1910)

They did love as well as man and wife could do, not conversing together.

Geoffrey Goodman, Bishop of Gloucester (1583–1656)

My wife and I tried two or three times in the last few years to have breakfast together, but it was so disagreeable we had to stop.

Winston Churchill (1894–1965)

He gave way to the queer, savage feeling that sometimes takes by the throat a husband twenty years married, when he sees, across the table, the same face of his wedded wife, and knows that, as he has sat facing it, so must he continue to sit until the day of its death or his own.

Rudyard Kipling (1865–1936) *The Brocklehurst Divorce Case*

Nancy Astor: If I were your wife, I would put poison in your coffee.
Winston Churchill: Nancy, if I were your husband, I would drink it.

It destroys one's nerves to be amiable every day to the same human being.

Benjamin Disraeli (1804–1881)

Marriage from love – like vinegar from wine –
A sad, sour, sober beverage – by time
Is sharpened from its high celestial flavour,
Down to a very homely household savour.

George Gordon, Lord Byron (1788–1824) *Don Juan*

When you're young, you think of marriage as a train you simply have to catch. You run and run until you've caught it, and then you sit back and look out of the window and realize you're bored.

Elizabeth Bowen (1899–1973) in conversation

I cannot prefer the awful eternal presence of marriage to the magic of meetings and partings.

Iris Murdoch (1919–1999) *The Sea, the Sea*

Oh! How many torments lie in the small circle of a wedding-ring!

Colley Cibber (1671–1759) *The Double Dealer*

If it were not for the presents, an elopement would be preferable.

George Ade (1866–1944) *Forty Modern Fables*

I would be married, but I'd have no wife,
I would be married to a single life.

Richard Crashaw (1612–1649) 'On Marriage'

I am in truth very thankful for not having married at all.

Harriet Martineau (1802–1876)

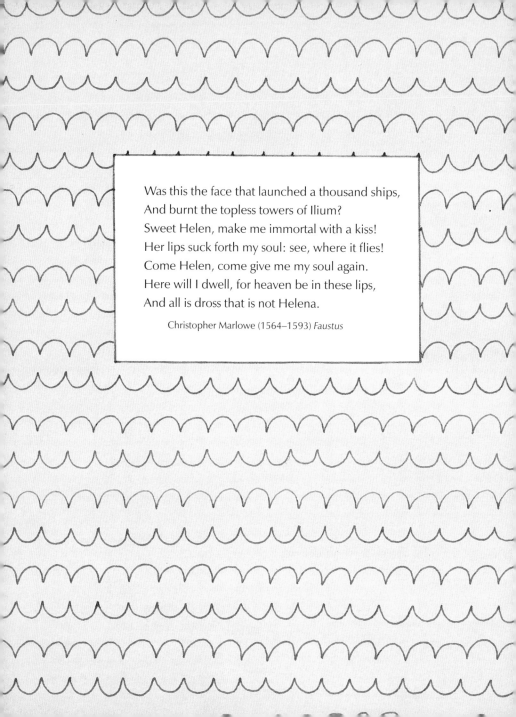

Was this the face that launched a thousand ships,
And burnt the topless towers of Ilium?
Sweet Helen, make me immortal with a kiss!
Her lips suck forth my soul: see, where it flies!
Come Helen, come give me my soul again.
Here will I dwell, for heaven be in these lips,
And all is dross that is not Helena.

Christopher Marlowe (1564–1593) *Faustus*

PART IV
The Love Affair

Anyone can be passionate, but it takes real lovers to be silly.

Rose Franken (1896–1988) *Another Claudia*

But love is blind, and lovers cannot see
The pretty follies that themselves commit.

William Shakespeare (1564–1616) *The Merchant of Venice*

We that are true lovers run into strange capers.

William Shakespeare (1564–1616) *As You Like It*

Yet for all this, amongst so many irksome, absurd, troublesome symptoms, inconveniences, phantasmagorical fits and passions which are usually incident to such persons, there be some good and graceful qualities in lovers.

Robert Burton (1577–1640) *The Anatomy of Melancholy*

If Cleopatra's nose had been shorter, the whole history
of the world would have been different.

Blaise Pascal (1623–1662) *Pensees*

Tristan, Isolde; Isolde, Tristan;
A man, a woman; a woman, a man.

Gottfried von Strassburg (13th century)

Good argument hath Peter in his head
But better hath he in his bed.

(Of Heloise and Abelard)

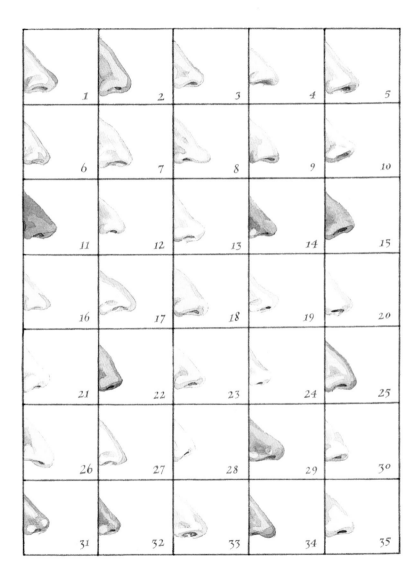

'Let us not speak, for the love we bear one another –
    Let us hold hands and look.'
She, such a very ordinary little woman;
    He, such a thumping crook.
But both, for a moment, little lower than the angels
    In the teashop's ingle-nook.

John Betjeman (1906–1984) 'In a Bath Teashop'

They loved each other beyond belief;
She was a harlot and he was a thief.

Lord Lytton (1803–1873)

Gallons of ink and miles of typewriter ribbon expended
on the misery of the unrequited lover; not a word about
the utter tedium of the unrequiting.

Tom Stoppard (*b.* 1937) *The Real Thing*

Werther had a love for Charlotte
    Such as words could never utter;
Would you know how first he met her?
    She was cutting bread and butter.

Charlotte was a married lady,
    And a moral man was Werther;
And for all the wealth of Indies,
    Would do nothing for to hurt her.

So he sighed and pined and ogled,
    And his passion boiled and bubbled,
Till he blew his silly brains out,
    And no more by it was troubled.

Charlotte, having seen his body
    Borne before her on a shutter,
Like a well-conducted person,
    Went on cutting bread and butter.

William Makepeace Thackeray (1811–1863) 'The Sorrows of Werther'

She deceiving;
  I believing;
What need lovers wish for more?

Sir Charles Sedley (1639–1701)

Follow a shadow, it still flies you;
Seem to fly it, it will pursue;
So court a mistress, she denies you;
Let her alone, she will court you.
Say, are not women, then,
Still but the shadows of us men?

Ben Jonson (1573–1637)

By the time you swear you're his,
Shivering and sighing,
And he vows his passion is
Infinite, undying –
Lady, make a note of this:
One of you is lying.

Dorothy Parker (1893–1967) 'Unfortunate Coincidence'

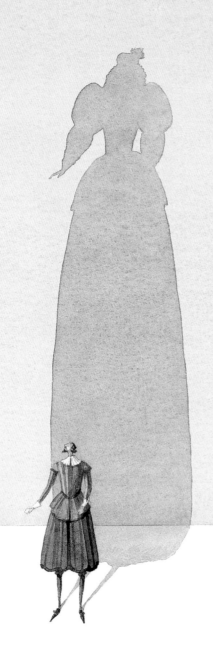

How can one e'er be sure
If true love will endure?
    My thoughts this morning are
    As tangled as my hair.

Lady Horikawa (Japanese, 13th century) translated by Curtis Hidden

I have always sworn to my lovers to love them eternally,
but for me eternity is a quarter of an hour.

Ninon de Lenclos (1615–1705)

Love is like linen, often changed, the sweeter.

Phineas Fletcher (1580–1650) *Sicelides*

Give me chastity and constancy, but not yet.

St Augustine (354–430)

All discarded lovers should be given a second chance,
but with somebody else.

Mae West (1893–1980)

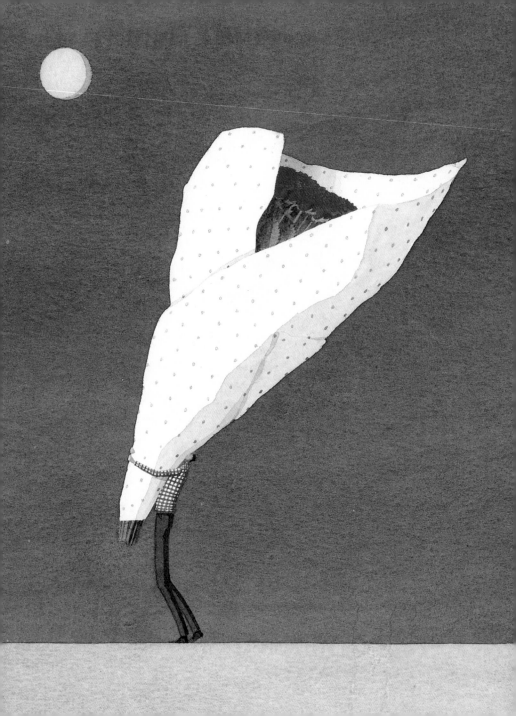

There is nothing better for the spirit or body than a love affair.
It elevates thoughts and flattens stomachs.

Barbara Howar (*b*.1934) *Laughing all the Way*

Adultery is hard work.

Xavier Marias *Todas las Almas*

Nuptial love maketh mankind; friendly love perfecteth it;
but wanton love corrupteth and embaseth it.

Francis Bacon (1561–1626) *Of Love*

Desire followed a glance, and pleasure followed desire.

Johann Wolfgang von Goethe (1749–1832) *Romische Elegien*

Lust is the oldest lion of them all.

Anonymous (Italy)

When he and I got under sheet,
I let him have his way complete,
And now my girdle will not meet.
Dear God, what shall I say of it?

Anonymous

Ah dear God, I am forsaken
Now my maidenhood is taken!

Anonymous

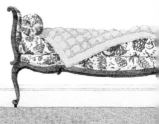

My true love hath my heart, and I have his,
    By just exchange, one for the other given.
I hold his dear, and mine he cannot miss:
    There never was a better bargain driven.
His heart in me keeps me and him in one,
    My heart in him his thoughts and senses guides:
He loves my heart, for once it was his own:
    I cherish his, because in me it bides.
His heart his wound received from my sight:
    My heart was wounded, with his wounded heart,
For as from me on him his hurt did light,
    So still methought in me his hurt did smart:
        Both equal hurt, in this change sought our bliss:
        My true love hath my heart and I have his.

Sir Philip Sidney (1554–1586)

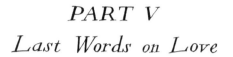

PART V
Last Words on Love

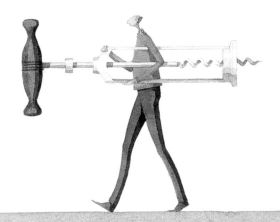

It is unfortunate not to be loved at all; but it is insulting to be loved no longer.

Montesquieu (1689–1755) *Lettres*

Take me or leave me; or, as is the usual order of things, both.

Dorothy Parker (1893–1967)

The day he moved out was terrible –
That evening she went through hell.
His absence wasn't a problem
But the corkscrew went as well.

Wendy Cope (*b.*1945) 'Loss'

When you are old and grey and full of sleep,
And nodding by the fire, take down this book,
And slowly read, and dream of the soft look
Your eyes had once, and of their shadows deep;

How many loved your moments of glad grace,
And loved your beauty with love false or true;
But one man loved the pilgrim soul in you,
And loved the sorrows of your changing face;

And bending down beside the glowing bars,
Murmur, a little sadly, how Love fled
And paced upon the mountains overhead
And hid his face amid a crowd of stars.

W B Yeats (1865–1939)

He would not stay for me; and who can wonder?
    He would not stay for me to stand and gaze.
I shook his hand and tore my heart in sunder
    And went with half my life about my ways.

A E Housman (1849–1936)

Woman much missed, how you call to me, call to me,
Saying that now you are not as you were
When you had changed from the one who was all to me,
But as at first, when our day was fair.

Thomas Hardy (1840–1928)

She lived unknown and few could know
    When Lucy ceased to be;
But she is in her grave, and, oh,
    The difference to me!

William Wordsworth (1770–1850)

He first deceased; she for a little tried
To live without him: liked it not, and died.

Sir Henry Wotton (1568–1639)
on the death of Sir Albertus Moreton's wife

Stop all the clocks, cut off the telephone,
Prevent the dog from barking with a juicy bone,
Silence the pianos and with muffled drum
Bring out the coffin, let the mourners come.

Let aeroplanes circle moaning overhead
Scribbling on the sky the message He Is Dead,
Put crêpe bows round the white necks of the public doves,
Let the traffic policemen wear black cotton gloves.

He was my North, my South, my East and West,
My working week and my Sunday rest,
My noon, my midnight, my talk, my song;
I thought that love would last for ever: I was wrong.

The stars are not wanted now: put out every one;
Pack up the stars and dismantle the sun;
Pour away the ocean and sweep up the wood,
For nothing now can ever come to any good.

W H Auden (1907–1973) 'Funeral Blues'

I should like to drop
On the hay, with my head on her knee,
And lie dead still, while she
Breathed quiet above me; and the crop
Of stars grew silently.

I should like to lie still
As if I were dead; but feeling
Her hand go stealing
Over my face and head until
This ache was shed.

D H Lawrence (1885–1930) 'Dog Tired'

O Western wind when wilt thou blow
That the small rain down can rain
Christ, that my love were in my arms
And I in my bed again.

Anonymous

To see coming toward you the face that will mean an end of
oneness is – far more than birth itself – the beginning of life.

Holly Roth (1916–1964) *The Content Assignment*

And what do all the great words come to in the end, but that? –
I love you – I am at rest with you – I have come home.

Dorothy L Sayers (1893–1957) *Busman's Honeymoon*

My heart has made its mind up
And I'm afraid it's you.
Whatever you've got lined up
My heart has made its mind up
And if you can't be signed up
This year, next year will do.
My heart has made its mind up
And I'm afraid it's you.

Wendy Cope (*b*.1945) 'Valentine'

I never saw so sweet a face
　　As that I stood before:
My heart has left its dwelling place
　　And can return no more.

John Clare (1793–1864) 'First Love'

His pains were o'er, and he sighed no more,
　　For he lived in the love of a ladye.

W S Gilbert (1836–1911) *The Yeomen of the Guard*

Love one another, but make not a bond of love:
Let it rather be a moving sea between the shores of your souls.
Fill each other's cup but drink not from one cup.
Give one another of your bread but eat not from the same loaf.
Sing and dance together and be joyous, but let each one of you
    be alone.
Even as the strings of a lute are alone though they quiver with the
    same music.

Give your hearts, but not into each other's keeping.
For only the hand of Life can contain your hearts.
And stand together yet not too near apart.
For the pillars of the temple stand apart,
And the oak tree and the cypress grow not in each other's
    shadow.

Khalil Gibran (1883–1931) *The Prophet*

The final word is love.

Dorothy Day *The Long Loneliness*

ACKNOWLEDGEMENTS

The compiler and Publisher would like to thank the following for permission to use copyright material: A P Watt Ltd on behalf of Michael B Yeats for a quotation from 'When You Are Old' by W B Yeats; Faber and Faber Ltd. for quotations from 'Loss' and 'Valentine' from *Serious Concerns* by Wendy Cope and 'Funeral Blues' from *Collected Poems* by W H Auden; Gerald Duckworth & Co. Ltd. for a quotation from 'Enough Rope' by Dorothy Parker; New Directions Publishing Corp. for a quotation from 'Marriage' (excerpt) by Gregory Corso from *The Happy Birthday of Death*, by Gregory Corso, copyright © 1960 by New Directions Publishing Corp.; The Random House Group Ltd for a quotation from *The Young Visiters* by Daisy Ashford, published by Chatto & Windus; The Random House Group Ltd for quotations from Spring Fever/Joy In The Morning/The Old Reliable/The Adventures Of Sally by P G Wodehouse, published by Hutchinson; Viking Penguin, a division of Penguin Group (USA) Inc. for a quotation from 'Unfortunate Coincidence', copyright 1926, renewed © 1954 by Dorothy Parker, from *The Portable Dorothy Parker* by Dorothy Parker, edited by Brendan Gill. Every endeavour has been made on the part of the Publisher to contact copyright holders not mentioned above and the Publisher will be happy to include a full acknowledgement in any future edition.